Much About Nothing

A Shakespeare Story

RETOLD BY ANDREW MATTHEWS
ILLUSTRATED BY TONY ROSS

ORCHARD

For Patrick, Penny and Leila, with love
A.M.

ORCHARD BOOKS
338 Euston Road, London NW1 3BH
Orchard Books Australia
Hachette Children's Books
Level 17/207 Kent St, Sydney, NSW 2000
First published in Great Britain in 2006
First paperback publication in 2007
This slipcase edition published in 2013
Not for individual resale
Text © Andrew Matthews 2006
Illustrations © Tony Ross 2006
ISBN 978 1 40780 979 3
The rights of Andrew Matthews to be identified as the author and Tony Ross as
the illustrator of this work have been asserted by them in accordance with the
Copyright, Designs and Patents Act, 1988.
A CIP catalogue record for this book is available from the British Library
Printed in China

Orchard Books is a division of Hachette Childrens Books,
an Hachette UK company.
www.hachette.co.uk

Contents

Cast List

Don Pedro
Prince of Aragon

Claudio
Companion of Don Pedro

Benedick
Companion of Don Pedro

Leonato

Governor of Messina

Hero

Leonato's daughter

Beatrice

Leonato's niece

The Scene

Sicily in the sixteenth century.

Sigh no more, ladies, sigh no more,
Men were deceivers ever,
One foot in sea, and one on shore,
To one thing constant never.

Balthazar; II.iii.

Much Ado About Nothing

In the house of Leonato, Governor of
Messina, all was fuss and flutter. The
governor's old friend, Don Pedro, Prince
of Aragon, and several of his captains had
stayed at the house some months earlier,
on their way to war. With the war safely
won, the prince had decided to visit again
on his return.

Shortly before Don Pedro's arrival, two lovely young women hurried down to the main courtyard of the governor's house. One was Hero, Leonato's only child, the other was her cousin Beatrice. Though the two were closer than sisters, they had little in common. Dark-haired Hero's innocent

blue eyes matched her
mild-mannered
sweetness. Beatrice
had fair hair, a sharp
mind and an even
sharper tongue.

"Lord Claudio
fought well, by all
accounts," Beatrice
remarked to her cousin
as they descended
a staircase. "You took
quite a fancy to him
last time he was here,
didn't you?"

"Just as you took a fancy to Lord
Benedick!" said Hero, blushing.

Beatrice rolled her eyes. "Benedick is
the most irritating man I've ever met!"

"Why?" said Hero. "Because he's as witty as you?"

"Because he *thinks* he's as witty as me!" Beatrice growled. "If he lived off his wit, he would die of starvation."

Hero and Beatrice reached the courtyard

and stood beside Leonato, just as the prince's party rode in through the gates and dismounted. Don Pedro was flanked by Claudio, whose brown curls glowed in the sunlight, and Benedick, whose mouth wore its customary cynical smile.

Behind them came
Don John, the prince's
half-brother, with his
servant, Borachio.

After embracing
Leonato, Don Pedro
stared in wonder
at Hero.

"You've grown so tall
while I've been away!"
he exclaimed.

Hero, who was gazing at Claudio, who
was gazing back at her, made no reply.

"Or have we grown shorter, my lord?" quipped Benedick. "Perhaps the heavy armour we've been wearing has squashed us."

"Why are you prattling on, Benedick? No one's listening," Beatrice said sharply.

Benedick mocked her with a bow. "Ah, Lady Beatrice, as scornful as ever!"

"That's hardly surprising," Beatrice said. "When I'm with you, I see so much to be scornful of."

She turned away, to follow Don Pedro and her uncle into the house.

Benedick nudged Claudio in the ribs. "Pity the man who marries her, eh, Claudio?" he chuckled. "*Claudio?*"

Claudio was glassy-eyed.

"Did you see Hero?" he murmured.

"Yes! Pretty girl, not as pretty as her cousin, but—"

"Hero is the most wonderful person in the world!" Claudio sighed. Benedick peered closely at his friend. "You haven't fallen in love, have you?"

"Head over heels!" Claudio groaned.

"Ha!" scoffed Benedick. "You'll be telling me you want to marry Hero next."

"If I don't, I'll never be happy again," Claudio said gloomily.

Don Pedro appeared at the door.

"What's keeping you both?" he enquired.
"Claudio is in love with Hero and wants to marry her!" declared Benedick. "My lord, the day you hear that I wish to marry, set me up as a target and shoot me with arrows."

"Is this true, Claudio?" the prince said.

"Yes," said Claudio. "I didn't notice Hero before, because I could think only of the war, but now I've seen her beauty, I can't live without her! What shall I do, my lord?"

Don Pedro placed a hand on Claudio's shoulder.

"Leave this to me," he said. "Leonato is holding a masked ball tonight. I'll dance with Hero and explain your feelings for her. If she feels the same, I'll ask Leonato for her hand on your behalf."

Claudio beamed.

Benedick muttered under his breath.

* * *

That night, the ballroom of the governor's house swirled with music and dancers. Claudio stood on tiptoe and peered anxiously at Don Pedro and Hero as they swept across the dance floor.

On the opposite side of the room, Benedick, in a hare mask, was in conversation with Beatrice, whose mask resembled an owl's face.

Benedick had adopted a strange accent to conceal his identity. Beatrice knew perfectly well who he was, but pretended that she did not.

"Won't you tell me your name, stranger?" she pleaded.

"Pardon me, but no," said Benedick.

"You're as provoking as Lord Benedick!" grumbled Beatrice.

"Lord Benedick?" Benedick said. "Who is he?"

"He's the prince's jester, and the dullest of fools," said Beatrice. "People laugh more behind his back than they do at his jokes."

"If I meet him, I'll tell him you said so," Benedick said.

"Please do!" said Beatrice, slipping away between the dancing couples.

Benedick was stung.

"So that's her opinion of me!" he thought. "A jester and a dull fool."

He frowned, puzzled.

"But why should I care what Beatrice thinks of me?" he asked himself. "We can't stand each other – can we?"

Meanwhile, Don Pedro presented Hero to Claudio, while Leonato looked on in smiling approval.

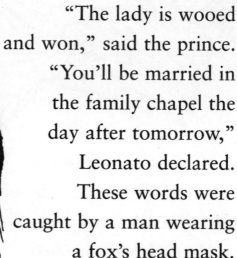

"The lady is wooed and won," said the prince. "You'll be married in the family chapel the day after tomorrow," Leonato declared. These words were caught by a man wearing a fox's head mask.

"My master ought to know of this,"
thought the man, threading through
the throng.

He was Don John's servant, Borachio.
As Don Pedro raised a goblet of wine to
toast Hero and Claudio,
Benedick chanced
by. He had
removed his
mask to reveal
a glum face.

"Celebrate with us, Benedick!" Don Pedro urged.

"Forgive me, my lord, but I'm not in the mood," said Benedick. "I'm escaping from Lady Beatrice. I've had enough of her for one night."

Don Pedro smiled at Benedick's departing back. "What a couple Benedick and Beatrice would make," he said. Leonato guffawed. "They would talk themselves mad inside a week!" "I suspect that they're fonder of each other than they realise," said Don Pedro.

"If we convinced Benedick that Beatrice was in love with him, and Beatrice that Benedick loved her, nature would do the rest."

"But how could we convince them, my lord?" Claudio said.

Don Pedro lowered his voice, and the others huddled round like conspirators.

✳ ✳ ✳

Borachio discovered Don John skulking in his room.

"You should have come to the ball, my lord," Borachio said.

Don John scowled. "Watching the prince being flattered would have sickened me! Because our father married his mother and not mine, he rules while I serve. I daren't challenge him, but if I could find a way to hurt him and his fawning friends…"

"I may know a way, my lord," Borachio
smirked. "I've learned that Lady Hero is to
marry Lord Claudio. I've also learned that
Lady Hero's chambermaid Margaret is
sweet on me, and that's given me an idea."

"What idea?" asked Don John.

Borachio answered at length, and what
he said brought a cruel smile to his
master's lips.

Next morning, Benedick strolled through the governor's gardens, deep in thought.

"Why does love turn people into fools?" he mused. "A few days ago, Claudio was a courageous soldier, now he's a drooling lapdog. It will take a special kind of woman to win my love – beautiful, wise, witty, well-to-do. Where will I find someone like that?"

Benedick followed a path between two hedges, and from the opposite side of the hedge to his left, he heard Don Pedro chatting with Leonato and Claudio.

The subject
of their
conversation
stopped Benedick
in his tracks,
but the hedge
prevented him
from seeing the
twinkles in the
men's eyes as
they spoke.

"So your niece
Beatrice loves
Benedick,
Leonato?" said
Don Pedro.

"To distraction,
my lord,"
Leonato replied.

"It's pitiful to hear her at night, whispering his name and weeping."

"But she behaves as if she detests Benedick!" said Claudio.

"Pretence!" Leonato assured him. "She knows that if Benedick finds out that she loves him, he'll mock her for it. To avoid the humiliation, she keeps her breaking heart hidden."

"Should I talk to Benedick, and tell him to be gentle with her?" enquired Don Pedro.

"I don't know what to do for the best, my lord," Leonato confided. "I'm afraid that Beatrice's passion for Benedick will drive her out of her wits."

The three men sighed heavily.

"Let's go inside," said Don Pedro. "A good idea might come to us over dinner."

For several minutes Benedick paced
up and down, chin in hand, while his
mind churned.

"Beatrice loves me!" he thought. "Poor
girl, I can't stand by and watch her suffer.
She must be rescued, and the only rescue
is…for me to woo her!"

"Benedick?" said a voice.

Benedick looked
round and saw
Beatrice behind
him. He
searched her
face for signs
of secret love.

"The prince
sent me to ask
you in to dinner,"
Beatrice said.

"It wasn't my idea. I don't care whether you have dinner or go without."

"Thank you for taking the trouble to find me," said Benedick.

"If it had been any trouble, I wouldn't have bothered!" Beatrice snapped.

She turned on her heel and flounced off.

"*If it had been any trouble, I wouldn't have bothered*," Benedick repeated softly. "There's a hidden meaning in those words...somewhere. She loves me, sure as can be!"

It did not occur to him to wonder why he felt so delighted.

On her way back to the house, Beatrice noticed Hero and her maid Ursula seated on the edge of a fountain that was ringed by statues on pedestals. Beatrice went to

join them, but ducked
behind the nearest
statue when Ursula
shrieked, "Lord
Benedick? In love
with Lady Beatrice?"

"Don Pedro told me
so," said Hero. "He asked me
to mention it to Beatrice, but I refused.
She'll never return Benedick's love."

"Why ever not?" Ursula exclaimed.
"He's a handsome enough fellow."

"Beatrice is too cold and proud to

surrender herself to any man," said Hero.
"If she knew about Benedick, she would
make a laughing stock of him, no matter
how sick with love he is."

"True!" Ursula agreed. "Better for the
poor man to die from love than from the
lashing of Lady Beatrice's tongue."

Beatrice's eyes bulged.

"Cold, proud – *me*?" she thought. "I'll show them how wrong they are. I'll save Benedick's life – by loving him. Don't die yet, dearest Benedick!"

She had never thought of Benedick as *dearest* before.

* * *

Late that night, Don Pedro answered a knock on his door and found himself facing his half-brother. "What is it?" asked Don Pedro. "Wake your friend Claudio," Don John said. "I have something to show him."

"At this hour?"

Don John nodded.

"If I told him, he wouldn't believe me, and nor would you," he said grimly. "You must see for yourselves."

* * *

On the morning of the wedding, all
Leonato's servants gathered outside the
family chapel. Hero looked radiant in her
wedding gown, Claudio and Don Pedro
seemed uneasy in their smart uniforms.

Benedick and Beatrice kept glancing at
each other and smiling.

The family priest, Friar Francis, raised
his hands for quiet.

"Friends!" he said.
"If anyone knows
of a reason why
this man and
this woman
should not be
married, then—"

"I know a reason!"
Claudio interrupted.
He pointed at Hero.
"She is dishonourable. Last night I saw
her embracing another man."

42

"You are mistaken!" shouted Leonato.

"No mistake, old friend," said Don Pedro. "I saw her too. She was on her balcony, kissing Borachio, Don John's servant. Claudio and I can no longer stay in this house."

Without a sound, Hero fainted and collapsed in her father's arms. Beatrice and Benedick hastened to assist her, while uproar broke out among the servants.

Don Pedro
and Claudio
marched in step
through the
clamour.
Leonato's eyes
were dazed.
"Can it be
true?" he
muttered.

"No, Hero is innocent!" cried Beatrice.

"Of course she is,"
said Benedick.
"This is some
trick of Don
John's to
spite the
prince's
friend."

Friar Francis crouched down and spoke quietly to Leonato. "Sir, take my advice. Have your daughter carried to her room, and announce that she is dead. Claudio will pity her, and pity will rouse loving memories in him. After a few weeks, when she is restored to him—"

"Claudio doesn't deserve her!" snarled Beatrice. "He should be punished!"

Overcome with emotion, she scampered into the chapel with Benedick close behind.

Beatrice stood before the altar, tears coursing down her face.

"If I were a man, I would make Claudio suffer for what he has done!" she declared.

"I love you more than all the world, Beatrice. I can't bear seeing you so upset," said Benedick. "I would do anything to comfort you."

Beatrice glared at him through her tears.

"Then go to Claudio, tell him that Hero is dead, and challenge him to a duel!" she said fiercely.

✳ ✳ ✳

Don Pedro and Claudio were
collecting their horses
from the stables when
Benedick found them.
He ignored their
greetings, seized
Claudio by the
throat and slammed
him against the
stable door.

"Hero is dead!" he hissed. "Your accusations have cost an innocent lady's life. Name a time and place, and I'll fight you with whatever weapons you choose."

He released Claudio, who stared in bewilderment at Don Pedro.

"Hero – dead?" he whispered.

Cursing voices made the three men turn their heads.

Borachio, with his hands tied behind his back, was being led up to the governor's house by a local constable.

"What's this, constable?" asked Don Pedro.

"I arrested this villain at an inn, my lord," the constable answered. "He was drunk, and bragging about deceiving you and Lord Claudio."

Borachio hung his head.
"The woman you
saw me with last night
was Margaret, Lady
Hero's chambermaid,
dressed in some of
her mistress's old
clothes," he admitted.
"Don John paid me to do it."
"Where is Don John?"
demanded Don Pedro.

"He left at daybreak," Borachio said.
"I don't know where he was bound."

"I'll have him hunted down!" vowed
Don Pedro.

Claudio sank to his knees and covered
his face with his hands.

"Hero was innocent – and I killed her!"
he sobbed.

That night, a funeral service was held for Hero. Afterwards, Claudio and Leonato spoke.

"How can I gain your forgiveness?" said Claudio.

"Nothing will bring Hero back, but there's something you can do," Leonato said. "A poor relation of mine is anxious for his daughter to marry a nobleman.

She's a lovely girl, very like my dear, dead daughter. Will you take her as your wife?"

Claudio, too close to tears to speak, simply nodded.

And so it was that early next morning, Claudio went once more to the chapel to be married. He was met by Leonato, Don Pedro, Friar Francis, and Benedick and Beatrice, who were arm in arm.

"Where is my bride?" asked Claudio.

Hero emerged from the chapel.

"Here," she said.

Don Pedro drew a sharp breath.

"Can this be the same Hero who was dead?" he wondered aloud.

"She was only dead for as long as her innocence was in doubt, my lord," said Leonato.

Claudio's eyes glowed with love and wonder.

"Hero?" he gasped.

"Take better care of her this time, Claudio, or I'll have to challenge you again," warned Benedick. He turned to the friar. "Is there room for another couple in your chapel? I asked Beatrice to marry me last night, and she amazed me by saying yes."

Don Pedro laughed.

"Shall I set you up as an archery target, Benedick?" he teased.

"I'm already a target, my lord," said Benedick, grinning broadly, "and all the arrows that struck me were fired by Cupid!"

I do love nothing in the world so well as you:
is it not strange?

Benedick; IV.i.

Love and Lies in
Much Ado About Nothing

Between 1598 and 1601, Shakespeare wrote an amazing ten plays, including *Julius Caesar* and *Much Ado About Nothing*. There was obviously a great demand for new works by him.

Shakespeare probably took the Hero–Claudio plot from a story by the French writer Belleforest. It was common for Elizabethan playwrights to 'borrow' plots – sometimes from one another!

In *Much Ado About Nothing*, Shakespeare writes about the foolish way that people behave when they fall in love. This subject fascinated him, and he returned to it in play after play.

The play shows us how easily we can be made to believe that a lie is true, and that the truth is a lie.

Claudio's love for Hero is sudden and passionate. Convinced that Hero has been unfaithful to him, he cruelly rejects her in public on their wedding day. When he is told that Hero is dead, and that he has been tricked, he is plunged into a despair that does not end until he discovers that Hero is alive, and that her love for him is miraculously intact.

The love story of Claudio and Hero is overshadowed by the story of Benedick and Beatrice, the reluctant, sharp-tongued lovers. They have to be tricked into realising what was true all along – that they fell in love with each other the first moment they met.

Shakespeare mixes bitterness into the comedy: Claudio's fury; the seething resentment of Don John; but the audience is never in doubt that the story will end happily. Like the banter between Benedick and Beatrice, the play is a lively game, full of twists, turns and tricks.

Shakespeare and the Globe Theatre

Some of Shakespeare's most famous plays were first performed at the Globe Theatre, which was built on the South Bank of the River Thames in 1599.

Going to the Globe was a different experience from going to the theatre today. The building was roughly circular in shape, but with flat sides: a little like a doughnut crossed with a fifty-pence piece. Because the Globe was an open-air theatre, plays were only put on during daylight hours in spring and summer. People paid a penny to stand in the central space and watch a play, and this part of the audience became known as 'the groundlings' because they stood on the ground. A place in the tiers of seating beneath the thatched roof, where there was a slightly better view and less chance of being rained on, cost extra.

The Elizabethans did not bath very often and the audiences at the Globe were smelly. Fine ladies and gentlemen in the more expensive seats sniffed perfume and bags of sweetly scented herbs to cover the stink rising from the groundlings.

There were no actresses on the stage; all the female characters in Shakespeare's plays would have been acted by boys, wearing wigs and make-up. Audiences were not well behaved. People clapped and cheered when their favourite actors came on stage; bad actors were jeered at and sometimes pelted with whatever came to hand.

Most Londoners worked hard to make a living and in their precious free time they liked to be entertained. Shakespeare understood the magic of the theatre so well that today, almost four hundred years after his death, his plays still cast a spell over the thousands of people that go to see them.

Orchard Classics
Shakespeare Stories

RETOLD BY ANDREW MATTHEWS
ILLUSTRATED BY TONY ROSS

Orchard Books are available from all good bookshops.